Ask God!

A Prayer Journal with
Question Prompts to Guide
Your Conversation with God

Ask God!

A Prayer Journal with Question Prompts to Guide Your Conversation with God

BY

RHODE JEAN-ALEGER

Edited by Victoria Kutch

Published by:

McDougal & Associates

www.thepublishedword.com

McDougal & Associates is dedicated to the spreading of the Gospel of Jesus Christ to as many people as possible in the shortest time possible.

ISBN 978-1-964665-06-1 Trade Paper Version
ISBN 978-1-964665-10-8 Case Laminate Version

Printed on demand in the US, the UK and Australia
For Worldwide Distribution

DEDICATION

This journal is dedicated to our Lord Jesus!

Ask and it will be given to you; seek and you will find; knock and the door will be opened to you. For everyone who asks, receives; and the one who seeks, finds; and to the one who knocks, the door will be opened.

Matthew 7:7-8

ASK GOD!

Call to me, and I will answer you; I will tell you great things beyond the reach of your knowledge.   Jeremiah 33:3

At times, one might feel hesitant to pose a question to God, considering His role as our Creator, Sovereign, and the Beginning and End of all things. However, it is crucial to remember that God not only permits, but also actively seeks a personal connection with each of us. He not only welcomes our inquiries and concerns; His open line of communication is a source of comfort and reassurance, a tangible expression of His love and understanding.

We can reflect on the examples set by biblical figures, who, despite their deep reverence for God, were unafraid to seek His guidance through their questions. For instance, when Abraham interceded for Sodom, he asked God: *"Will you really sweep away the righteous with the wicked? Suppose there were fifty righteous people in the city; would you really sweep away and not spare the place for the sake of the fifty righteous people within it? Far be it from you to do such a thing, to kill the righteous with the wicked, so that the righteous and the wicked are treated alike! Far be it from you! Should not the judge of all the world do what is just?" The LORD replied: "If I find fifty righteous people in the city of Sodom, I will spare the whole place for their sake"* (Genesis 18:23-26).

When the angel Gabriel announced to Mary that she would bear a son, Mary asked the angel: *"How can this be, since I have no relations with man?" And the angel said to her in reply, "The Holy Spirit will come upon you, and the power of the Holy Spirit will overshadow you. Therefore, the child to be born will be called holy, the son of God"* (Luke 1:34-35).

When Paul encountered the Lord, he asked, *"Who are you, sir" And he said to me, "I am Jesus the Nazorean whom you are persecuting." My companions saw the light but did not hear the voice of the one who spoke to me. I asked, "What shall I do, sir?" The Lord answered me, "Get up and go into Damascus, and there you will be told about everything appointed for you to do"* (Acts 22:8-10).

In these examples, our ancestors showed inspiring strength and unyielding faith and trust in God's purpose. Their belief empowered them to seek His guidance without fear, even without complete understanding of Him. This unwavering faith kindled a growing sense of hope in the Lord.

Neglecting to seek insight into God's heart and desires for us is common, but this oversight leaves us vulnerable to the infiltration of the enemy's deceit, steering us away from God's intentions for us. When we seek, we must be receptive to God's voice. Creating a tranquil space in prayer and remaining open to hearing God's voice through others and good music can help us in this journey.

When we ask God questions, we must do so genuinely, with an open mind and a respectful and humble spirit. It's important to trust God, who sees our hearts and will answer us according to His perspective. His thoughts are not our thoughts, nor are our ways His ways (see Isaiah 55:8). Therefore, let us ask Him for the grace to have pure intentions through our questionings and to believe in Him enough to accept His answers and obey His will.

The *Ask God* journal is a tool for individuals seeking to enhance their spiritual connection with the Lord. It includes a collection of scriptures, thought-provoking question prompts, short prayers, and quotes to encourage you to seek "grace" for various things in your prayers. These resources are designed to provide you with guidance, helping you to deepen your prayer experience and explore the heart of God.

The questions are adaptable, allowing you to customize them to your own preferences. The journal also provides ample space for personal reflection without specific prompts, acknowledging and respecting the importance of your unique and individual spiritual journey.

HEARING GOD'S VOICE!

My sheep hear my voice; I know them, and they follow me. John 10:27

God desires to communicate with us day and night. He eagerly waits to share His heart with us. The Scriptures support this belief: *"My sheep know my voice, and they follow."* If God did not want to speak with us, He would not have said *"my sheep know my voice."* The more time we spend with God in prayer and in the Scriptures, the stronger our relationship with Him will be and the more we will recognize His voice. Developing discernment is crucial, as it enables us to filter out the other voices that are not from Him.

As noted in Habakkuk 2:1-2, the prophet positioned himself to hear from God, and God responded to him:

I will stand at my guard post, and station myself upon the rampart;
I will keep watch to see what he will say to me,
and what answer he will give to my complaint.
Then the LORD answered me and said:
Write down the vision;
Make it plain upon tablets,
so that the one who reads it may run.

The prophet Habakkuk eagerly anticipated and listened to the Lord's message. He encourages us to position ourselves in quiet places and use all our senses to discern God's words. The practice of journaling helps in recording the words He speaks to us and demonstrates our reverence for His communication.

DISCERNING GOD'S VOICE

There are three voices in our heads: God through His Holy Spirit, our own voice, and the voice of the devil, and we need to know the difference.

God's Voice

God communicates His will to us primarily through the Scriptures. Understanding and living in His Word is crucial, as it enables us to be obedient to His voice and discern His guidance in our lives. The Holy Spirit will not speak contrary to scripture. For example, the Word of God says you must tithe, so the Holy Spirit will not tell you otherwise.

God's love for us is evident in the way He communicates. He speaks according to His nature and character as a Father who loves and wants the best for His children. The voice of God and the Holy Spirit may convict us if we are doing something wrong, but God's voice is not accusatory or condemning. Instead, it encourages and enlightens us, bringing us peace and clarity.

God's communication is personal and tailored to each of us. I learned to recognize His voice by following the unique pattern He uses to communicate with me. I do not hear God's voice audibly, but He usually speaks to me in the depth of my soul and heart (it is a bit hard to describe). His messages are often something I would not say to myself or they represent an unexpected answer to a question.

Once, when I asked God a question, He responded with another question, teaching me to consider the questions I ask Him if I want answers. His responses always bring me a profound sense of peace, clarity, and self-awareness, showing me how much He values our individual relationships and comforting me in times of uncertainty.

God is creative and can communicate with us in various ways. We should be open to the diverse ways in which He speaks:

HEARING: God's voice can be audible or not:

I will listen for what God, the LORD, has to say; surely he will speak of peace to his people and to his faithful. May they not turn to foolishness! Psalm 85:9

SEEING: God speaks through images, physical things that are happening around us, or things that He reveals to us:

The ear that hears, the eye that sees – the LORD has made them both. Proverbs 20:12

Knowing: When we know what to do, where to go, and where God is leading us:

For "who has known the mind of the Lord, so as to counsel him?" But we have the mind of Christ. 1 Corinthian 2:16

FEELING: When we can feel what is going on around us or with other people:

At Lystra there was a crippled man, lame from birth, who had never walked. He listened to Paul speaking, who looked intently at him, saw that he had the faith to be healed ... . Acts 14:8-9

God also speaks through the Scriptures, through songs, nature, and other people, etc. Sometimes, God gives me a strong or affirmative sense of what I must do in certain situations. Those are the times He directs me without saying a single word.

Our Own Voices

Our inner voice may reflect what we want to hear when making decisions. It's crucial to turn to the Lord for guidance in such moments. Ask Him, "Is this message from You, Lord?" Also, consider whether there's a hidden motive behind this inner voice or thought. We must be honest with ourselves to distinguish God's voice from our own. In order to do this, it is essential that we set aside the desires of our hearts, emotions, needs, and wants to hear God's voice, letting Him control our emotions as He speaks to us.

Our voices may also be full of pride, lies, doubt, and confusion. When we are not sure which voice is talking to us or when we realize that we are confused, we must call on and rely on the Holy Spirit to lead and guide us. We must also try to find wisdom through the Scriptures, knowing that God's words are accurate. In the silence and stillness of our hearts, we can learn to meditate on God's words, hearing His voice to gain peace and clarity.

The Devil's Voice

Be careful! The devil is the father of lies (see John 8:44). His job is to steal our peace and create confusion. The devil's voice condemns, discourages, confuses, frightens, and causes fears and worries. He likes to attack our identities in Christ by instilling lies in our minds and hearts, such as "You are not good enough," "You are worthless," "You are not a good parent," "You will never be anything in life," etc. When such thoughts come to your mind, you must reject them and boldly declare the truth of who you are in Christ, such as "I am the daughter/son of the Most High God, I am loved and cherished by my Father in Heaven, and I can do all things through Him who strengthens me." In this way, you replace the devil's lies with the truth of God because you know that God would never speak to you in such a way.

Whenever the devil tries to instill fear in my heart or attack my identity as a daughter of God, I take proactive steps to counteract his lies. Through God's grace, I immediately reject the falsehoods, declare God's truth, and turn to prayer or listen to praise and worship music. This brings serenity to my heart.

The devil may also tempt us with offers of pleasure, worldly desires, or passions. For instance, you might encounter a lucrative job with a prestigious title, but taking it could mean sacrificing precious time with your loved ones and your spiritual well-being. While the job may seem alluring, it's essential to consider whether it aligns with your values and priorities. Ultimately, it's crucial to recognize and understand God's guidance to make decisions that align with His will.

Let us pray for the grace to hear God's voice. He wants to speak with you!

PRAYER: Lord Jesus, I ask for the gift of discernment and the clarity to hear Your gentle voice. Give me the grace to focus on You, so that I may not just notice, but also actively respond to Your voice and divine presence in all aspects of my life. Lord, I give You my heart, my praise, and my heartfelt gratitude! In Your holy name, I pray. Amen!

Date: _____

Have no anxiety at all, but in everything, by prayer and petition, with
thanksgiving, make your requests known to God. Then the peace of God
that surpasses all understanding will guard your hearts and minds in
Christ Jesus.   Philippians 4:6-7, NABRE

Ask God: "Lord, why am I anxious right now?" Then ask Him for the
grace to overcome your fears and anxieties.

_____

_____

_____

_____

_____

_____

_____

_____

_____

_____

_____

Let Us Pray: Lord Jesus, we seek Your grace to strengthen our hearts
with Your peace. Grant us steadfastness in adversities and hardships.
In Your name we pray. Amen!

Date: _____

_____
_____
_____
_____
_____
_____
_____
_____
_____
_____
_____
_____
_____
_____
_____
_____
_____
_____
_____
_____
_____
_____

I am confident of this, that the one who began a good work in you
will continue to complete it until the day of Christ Jesus.
Philippians 1:6

Date: _____

_____

_____

_____

_____

_____

_____

_____

_____

_____

_____

_____

_____

_____

_____

_____

_____

_____

_____

_____

_____

REFLECT: On especially difficult days, when you cannot pray, just say, "Lord, I thank You and praise You!"

Date: _____

Whatever you ask for in prayer with faith, you will receive.
                                                    Matthew 21:22

ASK GOD: "Lord, where do I need to collaborate with You?" Then ask
Him for the grace to collaborate with Him.

_____

_____

_____

_____

_____

_____

_____

_____

_____

_____

_____

_____

_____

LET US PRAY: Lord Jesus, I long to serve You wholeheartedly. Please help
me be Your disciple in all seasons of life. In Your name I pray. Amen!

Date: _____

_____

_____

_____

_____

_____

_____

_____

_____

_____

_____

_____

_____

_____

_____

_____

_____

_____

Rejoice always. Pray without ceasing. In all circumstances give thanks, for this is the will of God for you in Christ Jesus.

1 Thessalonians 5:16-18

Date: _____

_____

_____

_____

_____

_____

_____

_____

_____

_____

_____

_____

_____

_____

_____

_____

REFLECT: When God permits us to experience challenging situations, it is to prepare us for something greater. Just like gold refined in the fire, we are purified through the trials of life. Don't be discouraged or complain. Instead, pray fervently, submit to the Lord, and ask for guidance. You were made to be extraordinary!

Date: _____

But he should ask in faith, not doubting, for the one who doubts is like a wave of the sea that is driven and tossed about by the wind. For that person must not suppose that he will receive anything from the Lord, since he is a man of two minds, unstable in all his ways.

James 1:6-8

ASK GOD: "Lord, where do I doubt you?" Then ask Him for the grace to have unwavering faith.

_____

_____

_____

_____

_____

_____

_____

_____

_____

LET US PRAY: Lord Jesus, grant me the grace to believe in Your goodness and to believe that You will work miracles in my life. In Your name I pray. Amen!

Date: _____

_____

_____

_____

_____

_____

_____

_____

_____

_____

_____

_____

_____

_____

_____

_____

_____

_____

_____

_____

_____

_____

_____

I praise you, because I am wonderfully made; wonderful are your works!
My very self you know. Psalm 139:14

Date: _____

_____

_____

_____

_____

_____

_____

_____

_____

_____

_____

_____

_____

_____

_____

_____

_____

_____

_____

_____

_____

_____

REFLECT: When the world brings you down, remember that God is always lifting you up! Stay open to His blessings in your life!

Date: _____

It was not you who chose me, but I who chose you and appointed you to go and bear fruit that will remain, so that whatever you ask the Father in my name he may give you. John 15:16

ASK GOD: "Lord, where are You calling me to serve?" Then ask Him for the grace to say "yes" to His call.

_____

_____

_____

_____

_____

_____

_____

_____

_____

_____

LET US PRAY: Lord Jesus, help me say "yes" to Your grace and call. I am dedicated to walking with You every day of my life. In Your name I pray. Amen!

Date: _____

_____

_____

_____

_____

_____

_____

_____

_____

_____

_____

_____

_____

_____

_____

_____

_____

_____

_____

_____

Probe me, God, know my heart; try me, know my thoughts. See if there is a wicked path in me; lead me along an ancient path.   Psalm 139:23-24

Date: _____

_____

_____

_____

_____

_____

_____

_____

_____

_____

_____

_____

_____

_____

_____

_____

_____

_____

REFLECT: Stop holding yourself back with regrets from the past. Pray to break free from your mental prison and embrace the freedom that God created you for. Pray to let go of the past and confidently move forward into the present and future, knowing that with God's grace, you can conquer anything.

Date: _____

*One thing I ask of the L*ORD*; this I seek: to dwell in the L*ORD*'s house all the days of my life, to gaze on the L*ORD*'s beauty, to visit his temple.*
Psalm 27:4

ASK **G**OD: "Lord, do I make You my Lord and Savior?" Then ask Him for the grace to love Him with all your heart, soul, and mind.

_____

_____

_____

_____

_____

_____

_____

_____

_____

_____

_____

LET **U**S **P**RAY: In Jesus' name, I renounce the love of the world. I accept the Lord as my Refuge, Fortress, and only Savior. In His name I pray. Amen!

Date: _____

_____
_____
_____
_____
_____
_____
_____
_____
_____
_____
_____
_____
_____
_____
_____
_____
_____
_____
_____
_____

You are the light of the world.   Matthew 5:14

Date: _____

_____

_____

_____

_____

_____

_____

_____

_____

_____

_____

_____

_____

_____

_____

_____

_____

REFLECT: Let us unite to spread the life-saving message of the Gospel of light to every corner of the earth. The salvation it brings is for everyone, regardless of their background or beliefs. Sharing this message can bring hope and light to the world.

Date: _____

But if any of you lacks wisdom, he should ask God who gives to all generously and ungrudgingly, and he will be given it. James 1:5

ASK GOD: "Lord, what lies am I believing?" Then ask Him for the grace to believe the truth and to stand in His truth, light, and love.

_____

_____

_____

_____

_____

_____

_____

_____

_____

_____

_____

LET US PRAY: In Jesus' name, I declare that I am a beloved child of God, cherished and worthy of His unconditional love. I thank You and praise You, Lord. Amen!

Date: _____

_____

_____

_____

_____

_____

_____

_____

_____

_____

_____

_____

_____

_____

_____

_____

_____

_____

_____

_____

_____

My grace is sufficient for you, for power is made perfect in weakness.
2 Corinthians 12:9

Date: _____

_____

_____

_____

_____

_____

_____

_____

_____

_____

_____

_____

_____

_____

_____

_____

_____

_____

REFLECT: When the world tries to make you feel inadequate, always remember that God's grace is sufficient for you!

Date: _____

Until now you have not asked anything in my name; ask and you will
receive, so that your joy may be complete. John 16:24

Ask God: "Lord, am I a joyful person?" Then ask Him for the fruit of
the Spirit — joy.

_____

_____

_____

_____

_____

_____

_____

_____

_____

_____

_____

_____

Let Us Pray: Lord Jesus, fill me with Your joy and peace, for they are
my source of strength, even when my life seems to be falling apart.
In Your name I pray. Amen!

Date: _____

_____
_____
_____
_____
_____
_____
_____
_____
_____
_____
_____
_____
_____
_____
_____
_____
_____
_____
_____
_____

My soul, be at rest in God alone, from whom comes my hope. God alone is my rock and my salvation, my fortress; I shall not fall.

Psalm 62:6-7

Date: _____

_____

_____

_____

_____

_____

_____

_____

_____

_____

_____

_____

_____

_____

_____

REFLECT: Silence is not just the absence of sounds or words; it is a powerful tool that can help us clear our minds of worries and thoughts, leading to a peaceful and productive life. Therefore, it is crucial to ensure that our minds are not cluttered with concerns and fears. Prayer can help us create an environment of silence where God can shower the soil of our minds with His grace.

David, in his moments of despair, asked God when he felt forgotten by Him. This question, born out of David's deep sense of abandonment, resonates with many who have felt similarly in their spiritual journey.

How long, LORD? Will you utterly forget me?
How long will you hide your face from me?
How long must I carry sorrow in my soul,
grief in my heart day after day?
How long will my enemy triumph over me?
Psalm 13:2-3

Date: _____

Now to him who is able to accomplish far more than all we ask or imagine, by the power at work within us, to him be glory in the church and in Christ Jesus to all generations, forever and ever. Amen.

Ephesians 3:20-21

ASK GOD: "Lord, do I recognize all my blessings?" Then ask Him for the grace to acknowledge all His blessings and be grateful for His gifts and generosity.

_____

_____

_____

_____

_____

_____

_____

_____

_____

_____

_____

LET US PRAY: Bless the Lord! Praise to the Lord! He continues to bless us without ceasing. In Jesus' name I pray. Amen!

Date: _____

_____

_____

_____

_____

_____

_____

_____

_____

_____

_____

_____

_____

_____

_____

_____

_____

Not many of you should become teachers, my brothers, for you realize that we will be judged more strictly, for we all fall short in many respects. James 3:1-2

Date: _____

_____

_____

_____

_____

_____

_____

_____

_____

_____

_____

_____

_____

_____

_____

_____

_____

_____

_____

REFLECT: A teacher should lead by setting an example. If you teach others about sharing, you should share your belongings first.

Date: _____

Beloved, if [our] hearts do not condemn us, we have confidence in God and receive from him whatever we ask, because we keep his commandments and do what pleases him. And his commandment is this: we should believe in the name of his Son, Jesus Christ, and love one another just as he commanded us. Those who keep his commandments remain in him, and he in them, and the way we know that he remains in us is from the Spirit that he gave us. 1 John 3:21-24

ASK GOD: "Lord, am I just a hearer or a doer of Your words?" Then ask Him for the grace to obey His commandments.

_____

_____

_____

_____

_____

_____

_____

_____

LET US PRAY: Lord Jesus, strengthen my devotion to Your words and lead me to follow Your commandments faithfully. In Your name I pray. Amen!

Date: _____

_____
_____
_____
_____
_____
_____
_____
_____
_____
_____
_____
_____
_____
_____
_____
_____
_____
_____
_____
_____
_____

Be doers of the word and not hearers only, deluding yourselves. For if anyone is a hearer of the word and not a doer, he is like a man who looks at his own face in a mirror. He sees himself, then goes off and promptly forgets what he looked like. James 1:22-24

Date: _____

_____

_____

_____

_____

_____

_____

_____

_____

_____

_____

_____

_____

_____

_____

_____

_____

REFLECT: If you teach about serving, you should serve others first. By practicing what you preach, you can demonstrate the power of your message and inspire others to follow your lead. Therefore, let your actions speak louder than your words. Let us ask the Holy Spirit to help us become effective teachers.

Date: _____

I was ready to respond to those who did not ask, to be found by those who did not seek me. I said: Here I am! Here I am! To a nation that did not invoke my name. Isaiah 65:1

Ask God: "Lord, what is Your purpose for me?" Then ask Him for the grace to see His works in your life.

_____

_____

_____

_____

_____

_____

_____

_____

_____

_____

Let Us Pray: Lord Jesus, bless me with the wisdom to recognize my gifts and calling and the strength to accept Your purpose for me. In Your name I pray. Amen!

Date: _____

_____

_____

_____

_____

_____

_____

_____

_____

_____

_____

_____

_____

_____

_____

_____

_____

_____

_____

Be kind to one another, compassionate, forgiving one another as God has forgiven you in Christ.   Ephesians 4:32

Date: _____

_____
_____
_____
_____
_____
_____
_____
_____
_____
_____
_____
_____
_____
_____
_____
_____
_____
_____
_____

REFLECT: When facing indifference, don't be indifferent. Instead, make a difference by responding with kindness and compassion. It may not be easy, but it is the right thing to do.

Date: _____

The tongue of the wise pours out knowledge, but the mouth of fools spews folly.   Proverbs 15:2

ASK GOD: "Lord, am I keeping my tongue in check?" Then ask Him for the grace to center your conversation on Him and to keep your tongue in check.

_____

_____

_____

_____

_____

_____

_____

_____

_____

_____

_____

_____

LET US PRAY: Lord Jesus, please help me to control my words and speak graciously in every situation. In Your name I pray. Amen!

Date: _____

_____

_____

_____

_____

_____

_____

_____

_____

_____

_____

_____

_____

_____

_____

_____

_____

_____

_____

_____

_____

_____

But he was pierced for our sins, crushed for our iniquity. He bore the punishment that makes us whole, by his wounds we were healed.

Isaiah 53:5

Date: _____

_____

_____

_____

_____

_____

_____

_____

_____

_____

_____

_____

_____

_____

_____

_____

_____

_____

_____

_____

_____

_____

_____

REFLECT: Do you complain about your suffering? Jesus was stripped of His garments so that you may be clothed in His righteousness.

Date: _____

Then children were brought to him that he might lay his hands on them and pray. The disciples rebuked them, but Jesus said, "Let the children come to me, and do not prevent them; for the kingdom of heaven belongs to such as these."   Matthew 19:13-14

Ask God: "Lord, is my heart pure like a little child? In what area do I need to be like a child?" Then ask Him for the grace to have a pure heart.

_____

_____

_____

_____

_____

_____

_____

_____

_____

_____

_____

Let Us Pray: Lord Jesus, I pray that You create in me a pure heart devoted to You alone. In Your name I pray. Amen!

Date: _____

_____

_____

_____

_____

_____

_____

_____

_____

_____

_____

_____

_____

_____

_____

_____

_____

_____

_____

_____

Death and life are in the power of the tongue; those who choose one shall eat its fruit.   Proverbs 18:21

Date: _____

_____

_____

_____

_____

_____

_____

_____

_____

_____

_____

_____

_____

_____

_____

_____

_____

_____

_____

REFLECT: The value you place on a word determines its impact on you. Do not allow negative words to have power over you. Stay positive, no matter what!

Date: _____

Be kind to one another, compassionate, forgiving one another as God has forgiven you in Christ.   Ephesians 4:32

Ask God: "Lord, who do I need to forgive today?" Then ask Him for the grace to forgive them.

_____

_____

_____

_____

_____

_____

_____

_____

_____

_____

_____

_____

_____

Let Us Pray: Lord Jesus, I pray for the healing of my wounded heart. Please give me the grace to forgive those who have caused me pain and the ability to release any feelings of resentment, anger, or bitterness toward them. In Your name I pray. Amen!

Date: _____

_____

_____

_____

_____

_____

_____

_____

_____

_____

_____

_____

_____

_____

_____

_____

_____

_____

_____

*For I know well the plans I have in mind for you — oracle of the L*ORD *—*
plans for your welfare and not for woe, so as to give you a future of
hope.   Jeremiah 29:11

Date _____

_____

_____

_____

_____

_____

_____

_____

_____

_____

_____

_____

_____

_____

_____

_____

_____

_____

_____

_____

_____

REFLECT: *"Thy will be done"* is a beautiful and gentle reminder to trust God in all things. He has a plan for you!

Job asked God in his miseries:

Why did I not die at birth,
come forth from the womb and expire?
Why did knees receive me,
or breasts nurse me?
Job 3:11-12

I invite you to ask God questions about your suffering.

Date: _____

"My grace is sufficient for you, for power is made perfect in weakness."
I will rather boast most gladly of my weaknesses, in order that the power
of Christ may dwell with me.   2 Corinthians 12:9

ASK GOD: "Lord, where do I need Your grace at this moment?" Then ask Him for the grace to be receptive to His love and mercy.

_____

_____

_____

_____

_____

_____

_____

_____

_____

_____

LET US PRAY: Lord Jesus, I cannot live life without Your grace. I need more of it daily. Thank You for the constant outpouring of grace into my life. In Your name I pray. Amen!

Date: _____

_____

_____

_____

_____

_____

_____

_____

_____

_____

_____

_____

_____

_____

_____

_____

_____

_____

_____

_____

With all prayer and supplication, pray at every opportunity in the Spirit. To that end, be watchful with all perseverance and supplication for all the holy ones. Ephesians 6:18

Date: _____

_____
_____
_____
_____
_____
_____
_____
_____
_____
_____
_____
_____
_____
_____
_____
_____
_____
_____
_____

REFLECT: Someone has wisely said, "Bloom where you are planted." Refuse to let the world put you down. Say yes to God's gifts and use them to the fullest wherever you are.

Date: _____

"You shall love the Lord your God with all your heart, with all your soul, with all your mind, and with all your strength." The second is this: "You shall love your neighbor as yourself." There is no other commandment greater than these."　　　　　Mark 12:30-31

ASK GOD: "Lord, who do I need to show love today? Do I love my neighbor as myself?"

_____

_____

_____

_____

_____

_____

_____

_____

_____

_____

_____

LET US PRAY: Lord, give me the grace to love You above all things. Increase my capacity to love others. In Your name I pray. Amen!

Date: _____

_____

_____

_____

_____

_____

_____

_____

_____

_____

_____

_____

_____

_____

_____

_____

_____

_____

_____

_____

The LORD answered: I will make all my goodness pass before you, and I will proclaim my name, "LORD," before you; I who show favor to whom I will, I who grant mercy to whom I will. Exodus 33:19

Date: _____

_____

_____

_____

_____

_____

_____

_____

_____

_____

_____

_____

_____

_____

_____

_____

_____

_____

_____

_____

_____

_____

REFLECT: If you can ask God to be merciful to you, then you can also be merciful to others.

Date: _____

You are the light of the world. A city set on a mountain cannot be hidden. Nor do they light a lamp and then put it under a bushel basket; it is set on a lampstand, where it gives light to all in the house. Just so, your light must shine before others, that they may see your good deeds and glorify your heavenly Father. Matthew 5:14-16

ASK GOD: "Lord, where are You calling me to be a light?" Then ask Him for the grace to be a light in your world.

_____

_____

_____

_____

_____

_____

_____

_____

_____

_____

_____

LET US PRAY: Lord Jesus, help me to be Your light whenever I go. In Your name I pray. Amen!

Date: _____

_____

_____

_____

_____

_____

_____

_____

_____

_____

_____

_____

_____

_____

_____

_____

_____

_____

_____

_____

Put on then, as God's chosen ones, holy and beloved, heartfelt compassion, kindness, humility, gentleness, and patience.

Colossians 3:12

Date: _____

_____

_____

_____

_____

_____

_____

_____

_____

_____

_____

_____

_____

_____

_____

_____

_____

_____

_____

_____

_____

REFLECT: If you ask God for grace, are you showing grace to others?

Date: _____

If we acknowledge our sins, he is faithful and just and will forgive our
sins and cleanse us from every wrongdoing. 1 John 1:9

Ask God: "Lord, what is stopping me from confessing my sins?" Then
ask Him for the grace to humbly confess them.

_____

_____

_____

_____

_____

_____

_____

_____

_____

_____

_____

_____

_____

Let Us Pray: Lord Jesus, grant me the grace to confess my sins without
shame. In Your name I pray. Amen!

Date: _____

A mild answer turns back wrath, but a harsh word stirs up anger.
Proverbs 15:1

Date: _____

_____

_____

_____

_____

_____

_____

_____

_____

_____

_____

_____

_____

_____

_____

_____

_____

_____

_____

Forgiveness is a choice that is necessary to free ourselves from anger, bitterness, and past hurts.

Date: _____

You set a table before me in front of my enemies; You anoint my head
with oil; my cup overflows. Psalm 23:5

Ask God: "Lord, how does Your anointing look on me?" Then ask Him
for the grace to see His anointing upon your life.

_____

_____

_____

_____

_____

_____

_____

_____

_____

_____

_____

_____

_____

_____

Let Us Pray: Lord Jesus, thank You for Your anointing in my life. I want
more of You, Lord. In Your name I pray. Amen!

Date: _____

_____

_____

_____

_____

_____

_____

_____

_____

_____

_____

_____

_____

_____

_____

_____

_____

_____

_____

_____

_____

_____

_____

Give us today our daily bread; and forgive us our debts, as we forgive our debtors. Matthew 6:11-12

Date: _____

_____

_____

_____

_____

_____

_____

_____

_____

_____

_____

_____

_____

_____

_____

_____

_____

_____

REFLECT: Have you ever felt the need to retaliate for the wrongdoings of others? If yes, surrender your right to retaliate to the Lord. Vengeance is His.

Date: _____

No trial has come to you but what is human. God is faithful and will not let you be tried beyond your strength; but with the trial he will also provide a way out, so that you may be able to bear it.

1 Corinthian 10:13

ASK GOD: "Lord, where am I being tempted?" Then ask Him for the grace to fight the temptations in your life.

_____

_____

_____

_____

_____

_____

_____

_____

_____

_____

_____

_____

LET US PRAY: Lord Jesus, deliver me from all temptations and keep my heart fixed on You alone. In Your name I pray. Amen!

Date: _____

_____

_____

_____

_____

_____

_____

_____

_____

_____

_____

_____

_____

_____

_____

_____

_____

_____

_____

_____

_____

_____

_____

Be still and know that I am God! I am exalted among the nations, exalted on the earth. Psalm 46:11

Date: _____

_____

_____

_____

_____

_____

_____

_____

_____

_____

_____

_____

_____

_____

_____

_____

_____

_____

_____

_____

_____

Serenity of the heart comes from freedom from anger, bitterness, and
unforgiveness. It also comes from God's peace and joy and the love
of others.

Date: _____

Peace I leave with you; my peace I give to you. Not as the world gives do I give it to you. Do not let your hearts be troubled or afraid.

John 14:27

ASK GOD: "Lord, am I at peace with who I am?" Then ask Him for the grace to be a peace with yourself.

_____

_____

_____

_____

_____

_____

_____

_____

_____

_____

_____

LET US PRAY: Lord Jesus, please help me accept who You created me to be. Thank You for making me fearfully and wonderfully. In Your name I pray. Amen!

Date: _____

_____

_____

_____

_____

_____

_____

_____

_____

_____

_____

_____

_____

_____

_____

_____

_____

_____

_____

_____

_____

_____

_____

He [Jesus] said to her, "Daughter, your faith has saved you. Go in peace and be cured of your affliction." Mark 5:34

Date: _____

_____

_____

_____

_____

_____

_____

_____

_____

_____

_____

_____

_____

_____

_____

_____

_____

_____

_____

REFLECT: How far will you go to touch the Lord to be healed? Are you willing to touch Him like the woman with the issue of blood in the Bible (see Luke 8:43-48)?

Date: _____

For where jealousy and selfish ambition exist, there is disorder and every foul practice. James 3:16

ASK GOD: "Lord, in what area do I have bitter envy or jealousy toward my neighbor?" Then ask Him for the grace to repent from bitter envy or jealousy toward others and to love them as yourself.

_____

_____

_____

_____

_____

_____

_____

_____

_____

_____

_____

LET US PRAY: Lord Jesus, I consciously renounce envy and jealousy toward my neighbor. Please increase my capacity to love others as myself and to not compare myself with others. In Your name I pray. Amen!

Date: _____

_____

_____

_____

_____

_____

_____

_____

_____

_____

_____

_____

_____

_____

_____

_____

_____

_____

_____

_____

Your word is a lamp for my feet, a light for my path.

Psalm 119:105

Date: _____

_____

_____

_____

_____

_____

_____

_____

_____

_____

_____

_____

_____

_____

_____

_____

_____

_____

_____

_____

_____

REFLECT: When you feel anxious and worried, ponder the words of God.

When God summoned Moses to go to Pharaoh to deliver His people, Moses asked God:

Now, go! I am sending you to Pharaoh to bring my people, the Israelites, out of Egypt.
But Moses said to God, "Who am I that I should go to Pharaoh and bring the Israelites out of Egypt?"
God answered: "I will be with you; and this will be your sign that I have sent you. When you have brought the people out of Egypt, you will serve God at this mountain."
Exodus 3:10-12

Date: _____

Remember not the events of the past, the things of long ago consider not;
see, I am doing something new! Now it springs forth, do you not per-
ceive it? Isaiah 43:18-19

Ask God: "Lord, of what past experiences do I need to let go?" Then ask
Him for the grace to let go of the past and embrace the present with joy.

_____

_____

_____

_____

_____

_____

_____

_____

_____

_____

_____

_____

Let Us Pray: Lord Jesus, I pray for the freedom to release the past and
embrace the present moment in communion with You. In Your name
I pray. Amen!

Date: _____

_____
_____
_____
_____
_____
_____
_____
_____
_____
_____
_____
_____
_____
_____
_____
_____
_____
_____
_____
_____

The LORD bless you and keep you! The LORD let his face shine upon you, and be gracious to you! The LORD look upon you kindly and give you peace! Numbers 6:24-26

Date: _____

_____

_____

_____

_____

_____

_____

_____

_____

_____

_____

_____

_____

_____

_____

_____

_____

_____

_____

_____

REFLECT: God blesses us every day. What are you willing to give to the Lord in return?

Date _____

Strive for peace with everyone, and for that holiness without which no one will see the Lord. Hebrews 12:14

ASK GOD: "Lord, am I a person who cultivates peace?" Then ask Him for the grace to pursue peace at all times.

_____

_____

_____

_____

_____

_____

_____

_____

_____

_____

_____

_____

_____

LET US PRAY: Lord Jesus, help me share Your peace wherever I go. Teach me to seek Your peace when adversity comes. In Your name I pray. Amen!

Date: _____

_____

_____

_____

_____

_____

_____

_____

_____

_____

_____

_____

_____

_____

_____

_____

_____

_____

Indeed, the word of God is living and effective, sharper than any two-edged sword, penetrating even between soul and spirit, joints and marrow, and able to discern reflections and thoughts of the heart.

Hebrews 4:12

Date: _____

_____

_____

_____

_____

_____

_____

_____

_____

_____

_____

_____

_____

_____

_____

_____

_____

_____

_____

_____

_____

REFLECT: Are you hungry and thirsty for the Lord? Then spend time in His Word and in prayer.

Date _____

For you did not receive a spirit of slavery to fall back into fear, but you
received a spirit of adoption, through which we cry, "Abba, Father!"
Romans 8:15

ASK GOD: "What are my fears?" Then ask Him to help you renounce all fear in your life.

_____

_____

_____

_____

_____

_____

_____

_____

_____

_____

_____

LET US PRAY: Lord Jesus, I come before You to renounce my fear of (name your fear). I ask for Your blessings of hope, love, joy, and peace to fill my heart. In Your holy name I pray. Amen!

Date: _____

_____

_____

_____

_____

_____

_____

_____

_____

_____

_____

_____

_____

_____

_____

_____

_____

_____

_____

_____

_____

_____

_____

With firm purpose you maintain peace; in peace, because of our trust in you.   Isaiah 26:3

Date: _____

_____

_____

_____

_____

_____

_____

_____

_____

_____

_____

_____

_____

_____

_____

_____

REFLECT: If you are not at peace with God, you cannot be peaceful within yourself. God is your Father, and He holds the key to your life. Therefore, pray and strive to restore and maintain your relationship with Him and to walk humbly with Him.

Date _____

When pride comes, disgrace comes; but with the humble is wisdom.

Proverbs 11:2

Ask God: "Lord, reveal my pride and help me embrace a spirit of humility." Then ask Him for the grace to turn from pride to humility.

_____

_____

_____

_____

_____

_____

_____

_____

_____

_____

_____

_____

Let Us Pray: Lord Jesus, show me my prideful behavior. Help me renounce pride and embrace the humility that comes from You. In Your name I pray. Amen!

Date: _____

_____

_____

_____

_____

_____

_____

_____

_____

_____

_____

_____

_____

_____

_____

_____

_____

_____

With all prayer and supplication, pray at every opportunity in the Spirit. To that end, be watchful with all perseverance and supplication for all the holy ones. Ephesians 6:18

Date: _____

_____

_____

_____

_____

_____

_____

_____

_____

_____

_____

_____

_____

_____

_____

_____

_____

_____

_____

_____

REFLECT: Sometimes it is of utmost importance to remain silent amid discontentment, disagreements, disapproval, chaos, and troubles in order to receive the peace of God and maintain it within yourself and your environment.

Date _____

Cast your care upon the LORD, who will give you support. He will never allow the righteous to stumble. Psalm 55:23

ASK GOD: "Lord, in what areas of my life do I need to permit You to work freely?" Then ask Him for the grace to fully surrender yourself to Him.

_____

_____

_____

_____

_____

_____

_____

_____

_____

_____

_____

_____

_____

_____

_____

LET US PRAY: Lord Jesus, I surrender myself to You. Work through me, lead me, and use me for Your glory. In Your name I pray. Amen!

Date: _____

_____

_____

_____

_____

_____

_____

_____

_____

_____

_____

_____

_____

_____

_____

_____

_____

_____

May the eyes of [your] hearts be enlightened, that you may know what is the hope that belongs to his call, what are the riches of glory in his inheritance among the holy ones. Ephesians 1:18

Date: _____

_____

_____

_____

_____

_____

_____

_____

_____

_____

_____

_____

_____

_____

_____

_____

_____

_____

REFLECT: The poor may have more supernatural peace and joy than the rich, for the poor may focus on Jesus for everything. Hence, let us be reminded of Jesus' teaching: *"It is easier for a camel to go through the eye of a needle than for one who is rich to enter the kingdom of God"* (Matthew 19:24).

Date _____

The fruit of the Spirit is love, joy, peace, patience, kindness, generosity, faithfulness, gentleness, self-control. Against such there is no law.
Galatians 5:22-23

ASK GOD: "Lord, which fruits of the Spirit do I need to grow in my life?" Then ask Him for the grace for the fruits of the Spirit to grow in your life.

_____

_____

_____

_____

_____

_____

_____

_____

_____

_____

_____

LET US PRAY: Lord Jesus, I desire an increase in the fruits of the Spirit. Open my heart so that I can freely accept Your gifts. In Your name I pray. Amen!

Date: _____

_____

_____

_____

_____

_____

_____

_____

_____

_____

_____

_____

_____

_____

_____

_____

Behold, God's dwelling is with the human race. He will dwell with them and they will be his people and God himself will always be with them [as their God]. He will wipe every tear from their eyes, and there shall be no more death or mourning, wailing or pain, [for] the old order has passed away. Revelation 21:3-4

Date: _____

_____

_____

_____

_____

_____

_____

_____

_____

_____

_____

_____

_____

_____

_____

_____

_____

_____

_____

REFLECT: Plant peace in your heart so that it can bloom in your family, workplace, environment, and the world.

Date _____

Through him [then] let us continually offer God a sacrifice of praise,
that is, the fruit of lips that confess his name.   Hebrews 13:15

Ask God: "Lord, show me what I need to be grateful for today." Then ask
Him for the grace to be thankful for all His gifts and daily provisions.

_____

_____

_____

_____

_____

_____

_____

_____

_____

_____

Let Us Pray: I am sorry, Lord, for the times I forgot to thank You for Your
goodness and mercy. With all my heart, I thank You and praise You
for Your constant and vital involvement in my life. Help me never to
stop loving, thanking, and praising You. In Your name I pray. Amen!

Date: _____

_____

_____

_____

_____

_____

_____

_____

_____

_____

_____

_____

_____

_____

_____

_____

_____

_____

_____

His divine power has bestowed on us everything that makes for life and devotion, through the knowledge of him who called us by his own glory and power.   2 Peter 1:3

Date: _____

_____

_____

_____

_____

_____

_____

_____

_____

_____

_____

_____

_____

_____

_____

_____

_____

_____

_____

_____

_____

REFLECT: Trust in God's plan so you no longer worry when things don't go your way.

While John was in prison, he asked this question about Jesus:

When John heard in prison of the works of the Messiah, he sent his disciples to him with this question, "Are you the one who is to come, or should we look for another?"
Jesus said to them in reply, "Go and tell John what you hear and see: the blind regain their sight, the lame walk, lepers are cleansed, the deaf hear, the dead are raised, and the poor have the good news proclaimed to them. And blessed is the one who takes no offense at me."
Matthew 11:2-6

Date _____

Praise the LORD, my soul; I will praise the LORD all my life, sing praise to my God while I live.   Psalm 146:2

ASK GOD: "Lord, you have shown me unwavering faithfulness. Am I reciprocating with gratitude?" Then ask Him for grace to be His faithful servant.

_____

_____

_____

_____

_____

_____

_____

_____

_____

_____

LET US PRAY: Lord Jesus, life's many demands often pull me in different directions, making it a constant struggle to remain faithful in my walk with You. Help me, Lord, to remain steadfast in our journey together, regardless of the successes, trials, hardships or uncertainties of life. In Your name I pray. Amen!

Date: _____

_____

_____

_____

_____

_____

_____

_____

_____

_____

_____

_____

_____

_____

_____

_____

_____

_____

_____

Give thanks to the Lord, who is good, whose love endures forever.
1 Chronicles 16:34

Date: _____

_____

_____

_____

_____

_____

_____

_____

_____

_____

_____

_____

_____

_____

_____

_____

_____

_____

_____

_____

_____

REFLECT: Renew your mind daily with the Lord so that your identity in Christ remains unshakable.

Date _____

For freedom Christ set us free; so stand firm and do not submit again
to the yoke of slavery.   Galatians 5:1

ASK GOD: "Lord, what strongholds (addiction, lust, ungodly pleasure, greed, pride, vanity, worldly point of view of life, etc.) do I have in my life?" Then ask Him to help you break free from those strongholds.

_____

_____

_____

_____

_____

_____

_____

_____

_____

_____

_____

LET US PRAY: Lord Jesus, we give You full permission to free us from all strongholds hindering our relationship with You. Thank You, Lord, for Your inner healing and deliverance. In Your name we pray. Amen!

Date: _____

_____
_____
_____
_____
_____
_____
_____
_____
_____
_____
_____
_____
_____
_____
_____
_____
_____
_____
_____
_____
_____

I say, then: live by the Spirit and you will certainly not gratify the desire of the flesh.   Galatians 5:16

Date: _____

_____

_____

_____

_____

_____

_____

_____

_____

_____

_____

_____

_____

_____

_____

_____

_____

_____

_____

_____

_____

REFLECT: Deny regrets, sadness, and shame. Embrace your identity in Christ, your belovedness, joy, and peace.

Date: _____

Trust in the LORD with all your heart, on your own intelligence do not rely; in all your ways be mindful of him, and he will make straight your paths. Proverbs 3:5-6

ASK GOD: "In what areas of my life do I need to trust You more and worry less about the future?" Then ask Him for the grace to trust in Him with all your heart.

_____

_____

_____

_____

_____

_____

_____

_____

_____

LET US PRAY: Lord Jesus, grant me the grace to trust You with all my heart. Lord, let Your constant reminder that You hold my tomorrows in Your mighty hands bring me reassurance, so I shall not fear anything. In Your name I pray. Amen!

Date _____

_____

_____

_____

_____

_____

_____

_____

_____

_____

_____

_____

_____

_____

_____

_____

_____

_____

_____

Those trusting in the LORD are like Mount Zion, unshakable, forever enduring. As mountains surround Jerusalem, the LORD surrounds his people both now and forever. Psalm 125:1-2

Date: _____

_____

_____

_____

_____

_____

_____

_____

_____

_____

_____

_____

_____

_____

_____

_____

_____

_____

_____

_____

REFLECT: Pray for peace in difficult times and trust that the "Lord heals the brokenhearted and binds up their wounds" (Psalm 147:3, NIV). Believe in the Lord; He will restore and transform you.

Date: _____

Because you are precious in my eyes and honored, and I love you, I give people in return for you and nations in exchange for your life.
Isaiah 43:4

Ask God: "How do You see me, Lord?" Then ask Him for the grace to see yourself through His eyes.

_____

_____

_____

_____

_____

_____

_____

_____

_____

_____

Let Us Pray: Lord Jesus, sometimes I fail to see myself through Your lens. Help me see myself as You see me. In Your name, I pray. Amen!

Date: _____

_____

_____

_____

_____

_____

_____

_____

_____

_____

_____

_____

_____

_____

_____

_____

_____

_____

_____

_____

See, I am doing something new! Now it springs forth, do you not perceive it? In the wilderness I make a way, in the wasteland, rivers.

Isaiah 43:19

Date: _____

_____

_____

_____

_____

_____

_____

_____

_____

_____

_____

_____

_____

_____

_____

_____

_____

_____

_____

_____

REFLECT: God's supernatural peace is worth more than gold and diamonds. That peace helps us realize that God has control of everything.

Date _____

At that time I will deal with all who oppress you; I will save the lame, and assemble the outcasts; I will give them praise and renown in every land where they were shamed. Zephaniah 3:19

Ask God: "Lord, in what area of my life am I experiencing shame?" Then ask Him to help you renounce that shame.

_____

_____

_____

_____

_____

_____

_____

_____

_____

_____

_____

Let Us Pray: Lord Jesus, I ask for the grace to renounce and release any feelings of shame that burden my heart. Please fill me with Your boundless joy and grant me inner peace that surpasses all understanding. In Your name I pray. Amen!

Date: _____

_____

_____

_____

_____

_____

_____

_____

_____

_____

_____

_____

_____

_____

_____

_____

_____

_____

_____

Whoever loves discipline loves knowledge, but whoever hates reproof is stupid. A good person wins favor from the LORD, *but the schemer he condemns.* Proverbs 12:1-2

Date: _____

_____
_____
_____
_____
_____
_____
_____
_____
_____
_____
_____
_____
_____
_____
_____
_____
_____
_____
_____
_____
_____

REFLECT: Try to make peace in all circumstances, for peacemakers melt
the hearts of their enemies.

The ill-tempered stir up strife, but the patient settle disputes.

Proverbs 15:18

Ask God: "Lord, with whom do I need to be patient?" Then ask Him for the grace to be patient with others in all circumstances.

_____

_____

_____

_____

_____

_____

_____

_____

_____

_____

_____

Let Us Pray: Lord Jesus, You have been so patient with me. Bless me with the grace to extend patience and love to those who do not deserve it. I am grateful, Lord, for patience, this fruit of the Spirit. In Your name I pray. Amen!

Date: _____

_____

_____

_____

_____

_____

_____

_____

_____

_____

_____

_____

_____

_____

_____

_____

Make every effort to supplement your faith with virtue, virtue with knowledge, knowledge with self-control, self-control with endurance, endurance with devotion, devotion with mutual affection, mutual affection with love. If these are yours and increase in abundance, they will keep you from being idle or unfruitful in the knowledge of our Lord Jesus Christ. 2 Peter 1:5-8

Date: _____

_____

_____

_____

_____

_____

_____

_____

_____

_____

_____

_____

_____

_____

_____

_____

_____

_____

_____

REFLECT: Jesus let the peace of God the Father rule His heart during His trial and crucifixion. We must live by this example, allowing the peace of God to be part of our daily lives.

Date _____

Oh, that today you would hear his voice: "Harden not your hearts as at the rebellion."   Hebrews 3:15

Ask God: "Lord, how can I distinguish the voices that are not from You and how can I silence them?" Then ask Him for the grace to only listen to His powerful and guiding voice.

_____

_____

_____

_____

_____

_____

_____

_____

_____

_____

_____

Let Us Pray: Lord Jesus, help me discern the voices that are from You. Help me to only respond to the promptings of the Holy Spirit. In Your name I pray. Amen!

Date: _____

_____
_____
_____
_____
_____
_____
_____
_____
_____
_____
_____
_____
_____
_____
_____
_____

Then the LORD answered me and said: Write down the vision; make it plain upon tablets, so that the one who reads it may run. For the vision is a witness for the appointed time, a testimony to the end; it will not disappoint. If it delays, wait for it, it will surely come, it will not be late. Habakkuk 2:2-3

Date: _____

_____

_____

_____

_____

_____

_____

_____

_____

_____

_____

_____

_____

_____

_____

_____

_____

_____

_____

REFLECT: There should be no anxiety nor fear in those who are dying in Christ, because whoever believes in God shall not perish but have eternal life (see John 3:16).

When Jesus was crucified on the cross, He asked His Father:

And at three o'clock Jesus cried out in a loud voice, "Eloi, Eloi, lema sabachthani?" which is translated, "My God, my God, why have you forsaken me?"
Mark 15:34

Date _____

Encourage yourselves daily while it is still "today," so that none of you may grow hardened by the deceit of sin. Hebrews 3:13

Ask God: "Lord Jesus, how do You see (<u>insert a name</u>)? Please show me Your heart for them."

_____

_____

_____

_____

_____

_____

_____

_____

_____

_____

_____

_____

_____

Let Us Pray: Lord Jesus, help me to see others through Your eyes. Help me to love and to serve them as You do. In Your name I pray. Amen!

Date: _____

_____

_____

_____

_____

_____

_____

_____

_____

_____

_____

_____

_____

_____

_____

_____

_____

_____

_____

_____

_____

Proclaim a holy fast! Call an assembly! Gather the elders, all who dwell in the land, to the house of the LORD, your God, and cry out to the LORD!   Joel 1:14

Date: _____

_____

_____

_____

_____

_____

_____

_____

_____

_____

_____

_____

_____

_____

_____

_____

_____

REFLECT: Comforting those who are mourning is an act of goodness, love, mercy, and peace. Therefore, let us support, in words and deeds, those who need a shoulder on which to lean.

Date _____

Everyone who believes that Jesus is the Christ is begotten by God, and everyone who loves the father loves [also] the one begotten by him. In this way we know that we love the children of God when we love God and obey his commandments. For the love of God is this, that we keep his commandments. And his commandments are not burdensome.

1 John 5:1-3

ASK GOD: "Lord Jesus, what do You want me to do for You today?" Then ask Him for the grace to follow His commands.

_____

_____

_____

_____

_____

_____

_____

_____

_____

LET US PRAY: Lord Jesus, help me to do Your holy will all the days of my life. In Your name I pray. Amen!

Date: _____

_____

_____

_____

_____

_____

_____

_____

_____

_____

_____

_____

_____

_____

_____

_____

_____

_____

Go, eat rich foods and drink sweet drinks, and allot portions to those who had nothing prepared; for today is holy to our LORD. Do not be saddened this day, for rejoicing in the LORD is your strength!

Nehemiah 8:10

Date: _____

_____

_____

_____

_____

_____

_____

_____

_____

_____

_____

_____

_____

_____

_____

_____

_____

_____

REFLECT: Be self-possessed. Don't let others' negative words and actions affect your peace of mind and well-being. Instead, let God's words shape you to your fullest potential.

Date _____

In the same way, the Spirit too comes to the aid of our weakness; for we do not know how to pray as we ought, but the Spirit itself intercedes with inexpressible groanings. Romans 8:26

Ask God: Lord Jesus, how should I pray for this situation (<u>name the situation</u>) I am currently facing? Ask the Holy Spirit, our Advocate and Intercessor, to pray within you and through you.

_____

_____

_____

_____

_____

_____

_____

_____

_____

Let Us Pray: Lord Jesus, thank You for the gift of prayer, a powerful means of communicating with You. We acknowledge the Holy Spirit, who intercedes for us in our weaknesses. In Your name we pray. Amen!

Date: _____

_____

_____

_____

_____

_____

_____

_____

_____

_____

_____

_____

_____

_____

_____

_____

_____

_____

_____

_____

_____

_____

For God did not give us a spirit of cowardice but rather of power and love and self-control.   2 Timothy 1:7

Date: _____

_____

_____

_____

_____

_____

_____

_____

_____

_____

_____

_____

_____

_____

_____

_____

_____

_____

_____

_____

REFLECT: No one can give you peace but God and yourself. Therefore, strive for it, pray for it, and act on it!

Date _____

There are different kinds of spiritual gifts but the same Spirit; there are
different forms of service but the same Lord; there are different workings
but the same God who produces all of them in everyone.

1 Corinthian 12:4-6

ASK GOD: "Lord, what are my gifts and talents?" Then ask Him to make
those gifts visible to you so you can use them to the fullest for His glory.

_____

_____

_____

_____

_____

_____

_____

_____

_____

_____

LET US PRAY: Lord Jesus, thank You for the gifts of the Holy Spirit. Give
me the grace to fully use them for Your glory serving others. In Your
name I pray. Amen!

Date: _____

_____

_____

_____

_____

_____

_____

_____

_____

_____

_____

_____

_____

_____

_____

_____

_____

_____

_____

_____

Rejoice always. Pray without ceasing. In all circumstances give thanks, for this is the will of God for you in Christ Jesus.

1 Thessalonians 5:16-18

Date: _____

_____

_____

_____

_____

_____

_____

_____

_____

_____

_____

_____

_____

_____

_____

_____

_____

_____

_____

_____

_____

_____

REFLECT: Praise unlocks the doorway to God's heart!

Date _____

Blessed be God, who did not reject my prayer and refuse his mercy.
Psalm 66:20

ASK GOD: "Lord, what is preventing my prayers from being effective?"
Then ask Him to reveal to you anything that might be hindering your
prayers, such as unforgiveness, doubt, or lack of faith.

_____

_____

_____

_____

_____

_____

_____

_____

_____

_____

LET US PRAY: Lord Jesus, remove anything and everything from me
that is not of You. I pray that the prayers of my heart are acceptable
to You. In Your name I pray. Amen!

Date: _____

_____

_____

_____

_____

_____

_____

_____

_____

_____

_____

_____

_____

_____

_____

_____

_____

_____

For this reason, I remind you to stir into flame the gift of God that you have through the imposition of my hands. For God did not give us a spirit of cowardice but rather of power and love and self-control.

2 Timothy 1:6-7

Date: _____

_____

_____

_____

_____

_____

_____

_____

_____

_____

_____

_____

_____

_____

_____

_____

_____

_____

REFLECT: In times of need, turn to Jesus, who is always accessible and ready to help. Remember, His love is abundant, but you must ask to receive.

Date _____

To one is given through the Spirit the expression of wisdom; to another the expression of knowledge according to the same Spirit.

1 Corinthian 12:8

ASK GOD: "Lord, what specific word of knowledge or scripture do You have for me at this moment?" Then ask Him for the grace to hear His answer.

_____

_____

_____

_____

_____

_____

_____

_____

_____

_____

_____

_____

LET US PRAY: Lord Jesus, help me live in Your words, for they are the key to hearing You and seeing You. In Your name I pray. Amen!

Date: _____

_____

_____

_____

_____

_____

_____

_____

_____

_____

_____

_____

_____

_____

_____

_____

_____

_____

_____

But you, beloved, build yourselves up in your most holy faith; pray in the Holy Spirit. Keep yourselves in the love of God and wait for the mercy of our Lord Jesus Christ that leads to eternal life. Jude 1:20-21

Date: _____

_____

_____

_____

_____

_____

_____

_____

_____

_____

_____

_____

_____

_____

_____

_____

_____

_____

When faced with a dilemma, seek guidance by asking yourself: "What would Jesus do in this situation?"

Date _____

But when he comes, the Spirit of truth, he will guide you to all truth.
He will not speak on his own, but he will speak what he hears, and will
declare to you the things that are coming. John 16:13

Ask God: "Lord Jesus, what would You do in this situation (<u>name the</u>
<u>situation</u>)?" Then ask Him for the grace not to resist the Holy Spirit's
guidance and to open your heart to His direction.

_____

_____

_____

_____

_____

_____

_____

_____

_____

Let Us Pray: Lord Jesus, empower me with the courage to follow the
Holy Spirit's guidance even when it poses difficulties. I trust Your
wisdom and ask for the perseverance to stay true to Your will. In
Your name I pray. Amen!

Date: _____

_____
_____
_____
_____
_____
_____
_____
_____
_____
_____
_____
_____
_____
_____
_____
_____
_____
_____
_____
_____
_____

Lord, I am not worthy to have you enter under my roof; only say the word and my servant will be healed.   Matthew 8:8

143

Date: _____

_____

_____

_____

_____

_____

_____

_____

_____

_____

_____

_____

_____

_____

_____

_____

_____

_____

REFLECT: If God, Your Creator, can forgive you, who are you not to forgive yourself?

Judas, not the Iscariot, asked Jesus:

"On that day you will realize that I am in my Father and you are in me and I in you. Whoever has my commandments and observes them is the one who loves me. And whoever loves me will be loved by my Father, and I will love him and reveal myself to him."
Judas, not the Iscariot, said to him, "Master, [then] what happened that you will reveal yourself to us and not to the world?"
Jesus answered and said to him, "Whoever loves me will keep my word, and my Father will love him, and we will come to him and make our dwelling with him. Whoever does not love me does not keep my words; yet the word you hear is not mine but that of the Father who sent me.
John 14:20-24

Let your questions become your prayers, a transformative bridge between you and God, offering hope and solace.

Date _____

I will listen for what God, the Lord, *has to say; surely he will speak of peace to his people and to his faithful. May they not turn to foolishness!* Psalm 85:9

Ask God: "Lord, I eagerly await hearing from You today." Then ask Him for the grace to have unwavering faith when He communicates with you.

_____

_____

_____

_____

_____

_____

_____

_____

_____

_____

_____

_____

_____

Let Us Pray: Lord Jesus, empower me to trust in You when You impart Your message to me. In Your name I pray. Amen!

Date: _____

_____

_____

_____

_____

_____

_____

_____

_____

_____

_____

_____

_____

_____

_____

_____

_____

_____

_____

_____

_____

_____

He took away our infirmities and bore our diseases.   Matthew 8:17

Date: _____

_____

_____

_____

_____

_____

_____

_____

_____

_____

_____

_____

_____

_____

_____

_____

_____

_____

_____

_____

_____

REFLECT: Forgiveness is the language of love that acknowledges the need for forgiveness in oneself.

Date _____

One of them, a woman named Lydia, a dealer in purple cloth, from the city of Thyatira, a worshiper of God, listened, and the Lord opened her heart to pay attention to what Paul was saying. After she and her household had been baptized, she offered us an invitation, "If you consider me a believer in the Lord, come and stay at my home," and she prevailed on us.   Acts 16:14-15

ASK GOD: "Lord Jesus, how can I know You better?" Then ask Him for the grace to have an open heart toward Him.

_____

_____

_____

_____

_____

_____

_____

_____

_____

LET US PRAY: Lord Jesus, I desire a deeper understanding of You in my heart. In Your name I pray. Amen!

Date: _____

_____

_____

_____

_____

_____

_____

_____

_____

_____

_____

_____

_____

_____

_____

_____

_____

_____

_____

_____

I belong to my lover, and my lover belongs to me; he feeds among the lilies.   Song of Songs 6:3

Date: _____

REFLECT: When inspiration comes from God, the evidence is unmistakable.

Date _____

But God, who is rich in mercy, because of the great love he had for us,
even when we were dead in our transgressions, brought us to life with
Christ (by grace you have been saved), raised us up with him, and seated
us with him in the heavens in Christ Jesus, that in the ages to come he
might show the immeasurable riches of his grace in his kindness to us
in Christ Jesus.   Ephesians 2:4-7

Ask God: "Lord Jesus, I want to feel Your love more and more." Then
ask Him for the grace to feel His everlasting love, to have no doubt
about it, and to strengthen your relationship with Him.

_____

_____

_____

_____

_____

_____

_____

_____

_____

_____

Let Us Pray: Lord, I know You love me. Help me to strengthen my belief
in this truth within my soul. In Your name I pray. Amen!

Date: _____

_____

_____

_____

_____

_____

_____

_____

_____

_____

_____

_____

_____

_____

_____

_____

_____

_____

_____

_____

_____

_____

_____

_____

Rejoice in the Lord always. I shall say it again: rejoice! Your kindness should be known to all. The Lord is near. Philippians 4:4-5

Date: _____

_____

_____

_____

_____

_____

_____

_____

_____

_____

_____

_____

_____

_____

_____

_____

_____

_____

_____

_____

REFLECT: Do not give up on life; instead, surrender all to God!

Date _____

I charge you in the presence of God and of Christ Jesus, who will judge
the living and the dead, and by his appearing and his kingly power.
Proclaim the word; be persistent whether it is convenient or inconve-
nient; convince, reprimand, encourage through all patience and teach-
ing.   2 Timothy 4:1-2

ASK GOD: "Lord Jesus, how do You want me to share the Gospel with
others?" Then ask Him for the grace to share the Gospel as He leads.

_____

_____

_____

_____

_____

_____

_____

_____

_____

_____

LET US PRAY: Lord Jesus, help me spread Your message of salvation to
all I encounter. Give me the wisdom to know when I must preach in
deeds or words. In Your name I pray. Amen!

Date: _____

_____

_____

_____

_____

_____

_____

_____

_____

_____

_____

_____

_____

_____

_____

_____

_____

_____

_____

_____

_____

_____

_____

Put to death, then, the parts of you that are earthly: immorality, impurity, passion, evil desire, and the greed that is idolatry.

Colossians 3:5

Date: _____

_____

_____

_____

_____

_____

_____

_____

_____

_____

_____

_____

_____

_____

_____

_____

_____

_____

_____

_____

_____

_____

REFLECT: Remember this: God created you out of pure love. Therefore, it's a blatant lie for anyone to say that you are not worthy or good enough.

Date _____

In the morning let me hear of your mercy, for in you I trust. Show me
the path I should walk, for I entrust my life to you. Rescue me, LORD,
from my foes, for I seek refuge in you. Teach me to do your will, for you
are my God. May your kind spirit guide me on ground that is level.

Psalm 143: 8-10

ASK GOD: "Lord Jesus, show me the way to salvation." Then ask Him
for the gift of eternal life.

_____

_____

_____

_____

_____

_____

_____

_____

_____

_____

LET US PRAY: Lord Jesus, my desire is to receive eternal life on the last
day. Show me how to live a life acceptable to You so that I may receive the eternal life that You have promised, a promise that brings
me great comfort. In Your name I pray. Amen!

Date: _____

_____

_____

_____

_____

_____

_____

_____

_____

_____

_____

_____

_____

_____

_____

_____

_____

_____

_____

Let the word of Christ dwell in you richly, as in all wisdom you teach and admonish one another, singing psalms, hymns, and spiritual songs with gratitude in your hearts to God. Colossians 3:16

Date: _____

_____

_____

_____

_____

_____

_____

_____

_____

_____

_____

_____

_____

_____

_____

_____

_____

_____

_____

_____

_____

_____

REFLECT: When you allow God to lead you without any doubt and fear, He takes you to places beyond your imagination!

Date _____

Moreover, God is able to make every grace abundant for you, so that in all things, always having all you need, you may have an abundance for every good work.   2 Corinthians 9:8

Ask God: "Lord Jesus, I am grateful for Your blessings, goodness, and grace." Then ask Him to fill you with more of Himself.

_____

_____

_____

_____

_____

_____

_____

_____

_____

_____

_____

_____

Let Us Pray: Lord, fill me with more of You. Help me to walk in the power of the Holy Spirit as I do Your holy will. In Jesus' name I pray. Amen!

Date: _____

_____

_____

_____

_____

_____

_____

_____

_____

_____

_____

_____

_____

_____

_____

_____

_____

_____

_____

_____

_____

I will proclaim your name to my brothers, in the midst of the assembly
I will praise you. Hebrews 2:12

Date: _____

The psalmist asked God this challenging question: Where are You, Lord, when I needed You?

Why, Lord, do you stand afar and pay no heed in times of trouble?
Psalm 10:1

I invite you to personally write your question to God, fostering a deep and personal connection with Him.

_____

_____

_____

_____

_____

_____

_____

_____

_____

_____

LET US PRAY: Thank You, Lord Jesus, for Your grace and unfailing love. In Your name I pray. Amen!

Date: _____

_____

_____

_____

_____

_____

_____

_____

_____

_____

_____

_____

_____

_____

_____

_____

_____

_____

_____

_____

Let everything that has breath give praise to the LORD! *Hallelujah!*

Psalm 150:6

AUTHOR CONTACT PAGE

You may contact Rhode Jean-Aleger directly in the following ways:

Email: Jaxprayerclub@gmail.com

Website: www.Jaxprayerclub.com

More great titles from Rhode Jean-Aleger

From HIM and
through HIM and
to HIM!

*Inspiration
for Every
Day of
the Year*

Rhode Jean-Aleger

ISBN: 978-1-950398-75-1, 5 X 8, 388 pages

DECLARATIONS OF VICTORY

Rhode Jean-Aleger

ISBN: 978-1-940461-46-5, 5 X 8, 86 pages